Cryptocurrency Simply Explained!

The Only Investing Guide You Need to Master the World of Bitcoin and Blockchain – Discover the Secrets to Crypto Projects Like ADA, DOT, XRM, XRP and Flare!

by Barry Johnson

The following Book is reproduced below with the goal of providing information that is as accurate and reliable as possible. Regardless, purchasing this Book can be seen as consent to the fact that both the publisher and the author of this book are in no way experts on the topics discussed within and that any recommendations or suggestions that are made herein are for entertainment purposes only. Professionals should be consulted as needed prior to undertaking any of the action endorsed herein. This declaration is deemed fair and valid by both the American Bar Association and the Committee of Publishers Association and is legally binding throughout the United States. Furthermore, the transmission, duplication, or reproduction of any of the following work including specific information will be considered an illegal act irrespective of if it is done electronically or in print. This extends to creating a secondary or tertiary copy of the work or a recorded copy and is only allowed with the express written consent from the Publisher. All additional rights reserved. The information in the following pages is broadly considered a truthful and accurate account of facts and as such, any inattention, use, or misuse of the information in question by the reader will render any resulting actions solely under their purview. There are no scenarios in which the publisher or the original author of this work can be in any fashion deemed liable for any hardship or damages that may befall them after undertaking information described herein.

Additionally, the information in the following pages is intended only for informational purposes and should thus be thought of as universal. As befitting its nature, it is presented without assurance regarding its prolonged validity or interim quality. Trademarks that are mentioned are done without written consent and can in no way be considered an endorsement from the trademark holder.

Table of Contents

Introduction

itcoin has taken the world by storm once again when it crossed $20,000 per BTC in December of last year. After more than 2 years of bear market, the most famous cryptocurrency surpassed its previous all time high.

A lot of people are now trying to improvise themselves as professional investors and are losing a lot of money, only helping those who actually know what they are doing accumulate an incredible amount of wealth that will lead to generational fortunes.

To join the club of the few investors that actually make it, you need the right knowledge and the right mindset. Notice how we did not include a large initial capital. In fact, while having more money to invest means having more fire power, it is not necessary to have thousands of dollars to accumulate cryptocurrency and build wealth.

In fact, when we started investing in cryptocurrency we only had a few hundreds to put into the market, but that sum yielded us thousands and thousands of dollars over the span of a few years.

In this book you are going to discover everything there is to know about the fascinating world of cryptocurrency. From the operation of the Bitcoin blockchain to more advanced projects, like Uniswap and Compound.
If you diligently study the content of this book, we are sure you are going to see take your crypto knowledge to the next level. This also means you are going to see amazing results in a relative short period of time, since this bull run is offering an amazing number of opportunities.

To your success!

Barry Johnson

Chapter 1

Cardano (ADA)

Cardano and its related cryptocurrency ADA have attracted a lot of attention since its creation in 2015. The academic rigor applied to its development makes Cardano a rather unique project in the cryptocurrency industry.

The Cardano project is mainly developed by the technology company Input Output Hong Kong (IOHK), founded by Charles Hoskinson. Hoskinson also took part in the Ethereum development in its early days. But what is Cardano, and what are the features it plans to introduce in its long roadmap? Let's find out.

What is Cardano (ADA)?

Cardano is a multipurpose blockchain designed on the basis of academic research. Its development is entrusted to a multidisciplinary team of engineers, mathematicians, scientists and business experts.

The development of the platform is always achieved by applying a scientific approach. According to its creators, the fundamental design principles behind Cardano are security, scalability and interoperability. Ada, Cardano's native currency, is used to perform operations on the Cardano blockchain, in a relationship very similar to that between ether and Ethereum.

Cardano development is separated into multiple operating units. IOHK manages the development of the Cardano protocol, while the Cardano Foundation oversees the project and EMURGO is responsible for commercial development and adoption. IOHK also had to do with the development of Ethereum Classic (ETC).

The roadmap

Cardano's roadmap consists of five main stages: Byron, Shelley, Goguen, Basho and Voltaire. Byron, the first phase, saw the rollout of the network and core features, such as ADA relocations. The Shelley hard fork occurred in 2020 and offered further steps towards decentralization. Currently the nodes are operated by the Cardano community, with staking pools managed by ADA owners.

As of April 2021, the blockchain platform is still unable to accommodate functional smart contracts. According to the roadmap, this feature will be introduced with the Goguen update. Following Goguen, the Basho update will focus on optimizing scalability and interoperability, and the Voltaire update will introduce a treasury system to address the governance issue.

How Cardano works

Cardano is designed as a "third generation" blockchain, with the aim of solving the scalability problems of the first (e.g., Bitcoin) and second generation (e.g., Ethereum).

According to proponents of this classification, blockchains of previous generations suffer from bottlenecks that fundamentally limit the capacity they can handle. This makes them an inefficient choice for widespread use globally. We can observe the varying transaction times of BTC and ETH to confirm this problem.

In the documentation, Cardano indicates the computational power of VISA as a comparison: the network handles an average of 1,736 transactions per second (TPS) with the capacity to handle up to 24,000 TPS.

Cardano aims to improve capacity in several ways. One of the most significant pillars towards this goal is the Proof of Stake consensus mechanism called Ouroboros. Ouroboros reduces energy costs compared to Proof of Work and at the same time offers demonstrable safety guarantees.

Cardano's Layer 2 solution for further scalability, Hydra, is named after the mythological creature. The basic idea is that capacity increases with each new node added to the network.

The hard fork combiner is another key feature of Cardano, which allows you to hard fork without interruption or the need to restart the blockchain. The success of the Shelley update is proof of the effectiveness of this approach.

The key functions of Cardano

As we have mentioned, Cardano's strong points are its academic and scientific philosophy. The team developing Cardano has published more than 90 white papers for the underlying technology. The project has a well-defined roadmap, and the network aims to achieve high levels of security, scalability and interoperability.

Although not yet operational, the Cardano blockchain will introduce the functionality of scalable smart contracts in the future. Developed with VISA as a competitor and hardware limitations as a theoretical goal, Cardano could have all the elements needed to be used as a strong revolutionary fintech project.

As with Ethereum, the possibilities of Cardano's use cases are vast. The blockchain only aims to act as a foundation layer upon which to build applications.

Despite the great promises, Cardano has yet to meet expectations. That is something common to almost all projects in the crypto sector with the exception of Bitcoin. Even though Cardano is ambitious, its development is relatively slow.

The ADA Token

ADA is Cardano's token, named after 19th century mathematics Ada Lovelace. 57.6% of ADA's offering was distributed through an Initial Coin Offering (ICO), in which Cardano raised $62.2 million.
The token is both a digital currency and a way to transact on the Cardano network (similar to the role of ether to transact on Ethereum).

Additionally, ADA holders have a share of the Cardano network, which can be used in staking pools to generate rewards.

How to store ADA

Developed by IOHK, Daedalus is the open source desktop wallet software of choice for storing ADA. It is a full node wallet, so it is necessary to download the entire Cardano blockchain, and every transaction is verified for maximum user security.

Among the light wallets, which do not require you to download the entire blockchain, we find Yoroi Wallet and AdaLite. Additionally, it is possible to store ADA on hardware wallets such as Ledger and Trezor through Daedalus, Yoroi Wallet and AdaLite.

Will this third-generation blockchain project succeed in becoming the dominant smart contract platform, or will it arrive too late to the market? Are there 4th generation blockchains that offer better performance and functionality? These questions remain open as Cardano progresses on its roadmap.

What we know is that we have invested in ADA at 0.18$ and we have profit targets at $3 and $5.

Chapter 2

Polkadot (DOT)

Polkadot positions itself as the next generation blockchain protocol, capable of linking multiple specialized blockchains into a universal network. With a strong focus on developing the Web 3.0 infrastructure Polkadot aims to destroy internet monopolies and distribute power into the hands of individual users.

While the blockchain has been called a revolutionary technology, there are undoubtedly disadvantages to be taken into consideration. Individual blockchains are unable to communicate with each other. Introducing interoperability between different chains could lead to data exchange and potentially more powerful applications and services.

In the past, developers have tried to "link" different blockchains. This process allows chain A to work with chain B and vice versa. However, connecting many blockchains at the same time remains an unsolved problem. The Polkadot team, and by extension the Web3 Foundation, are convinced that an elegant solution can be created in the coming years.

What is Polkadot?

Described as an open source protocol built for everyone, Polkadot claims to be the next step in the evolution of blockchain technology. It is a concept originally envisioned by Dr. Gavin Wood, the co-founder of Ethereum. The team wants to focus on security, scalability and innovation. To do this, the necessary infrastructure must be created not only to support new ideas and concepts, but to ensure adequate interoperability as well.

An individual blockchain in the Polkadot ecosystem is called a parachain, while the main blockchain is called the Relay Chain. The idea is that the parachains and the Relay Chain can easily exchange information at any time. You can think of parachains as similar to individual shards in the planned implementation of ETH 2.0.

Any developer, company or individual can launch their own custom parachain through Substrate, a framework for creating cryptocurrencies and decentralized systems. Once the custom blockchain is connected to the Polkadot network, it becomes interoperable with all other parachains on the network.

Building cross-chain applications, products and services should become an easier process with this design. So far, cross-blockchain transfers of data or assets have not been possible on a large scale.

The protection and validation of data across these different parachains is done through network validators, and a small group of these validators can protect multiple parachains. Furthermore, these validators ensure that transactions can be spread across various parachains to improve scalability.

The advantages of Polkadot

There are several reasons for developers to explore the Polkadot ecosystem. Due to the limited nature of current blockchains, it is clear that there are fundamental problems to be addressed: scalability, customization, interoperability, governance and upgradeability.

On the scalability front, Polkadot offers several features. It acts as a multichain network, allowing users to process transfers in parallel across several individual chains. This removes one of the major hurdles associated with blockchain technology today. Parallel processing is a significant improvement and can pave the way for wider global blockchain adoption.

Those looking for customization can take advantage of other features provided by Polkadot. At present, there is no "one blockchain infrastructure to tame them all". Each project has individual needs and requirements, and Polkadot allows each individual chain to optimize its design for this specific functionality. With the help of Substrate, developers can efficiently tailor their individual blockchains to meet the needs of the project.

When it comes to interoperability, the smooth sharing of data between projects and applications is an important factor. While it remains to be seen what kind of products and services this system will create, there are plenty of possible use cases. It can create a whole new financial ecosystem, with each individual parachain dealing with a particular aspect of the system.

Any community associated with a specific parachain will be able to manage their network as they see fit. Furthermore, all communities are crucial for the future governance of Polkadot as a whole. Collecting feedback from the community can provide valuable information to evolve projects over time.

Plus, Polkadot makes upgrading individual parachains really easy. There is no need for hard forks, as these events can divide communities. Instead, the native chain can be upgraded without friction.

The DOT token

Similar to most other blockchain infrastructure projects, Polkadot has its own native token. Known as DOT, it acts as a network token, just like ETH is the token of Ethereum and BTC is the token of Bitcoin.

This token carries out several use cases. First of all, it grants owners governance rights over the entire Polkadot platform. This includes setting commissions, votes on general network updates, and the launch or removal of parachain.

DOT is also designed to facilitate network consensus through staking. Similar to other networks that take advantage of the staking mechanism, all DOT holders are incentivized to follow the rules at any time. If they don't, they could lose their stake.

The third function of the token is bonding. This process is necessary when new parachains are added to the Polkadot ecosystem. During the bonding period, the involved DOTs are locked, and released at the end of the bond duration when the parachain is removed from the ecosystem.

Staking and bonding on Polkadot

Polkadot's approach to interoperability goes far beyond the simple exchange of data and assets. It is also a way to introduce new concepts, such as incentivizing honest token staking and bonding.

Staking of tokens on a blockchain network is not a new concept. Known as Proof of Stake, this consensus model works by rewarding users for staking coins on the network. With Polkadot, honest stakers are rewarded, while bad operators can lose the entire stake.

As we mentioned before, each new parachain is added through DOT token bonding. Bonding refers to blocking tokens on the network for a specific period of time. Unnecessary chains or abandoned projects will be removed, and locked tokens will be returned.

On paper, there are many things that make Polkadot attractive in the eyes of developers. It is an ecosystem dedicated to individual programmers, small businesses and large corporations. Having the ability to implement custom blockchains to meet specific needs, and update them seamlessly, is a new concept that could be invaluable to the entire crypto industry.

That said, Polkadot remains a very young ecosystem. Even though several projects are already under development, it will take some time before the first major blockchains are launched. According to PolkaProject, there are hundreds of projects under development, from wallets to infrastructure projects, tools, dApps and more.

As for DOT, the creators of Polkadot have stated that it is not a token intended for speculation. While it has monetary value on exchanges, it is primarily designed for the purposes we just described.

We have purchased DOT at $6 and it represents around 10% of our portfolio.

Chapter 3

Ripple (XRP)

Previously known as OpenCoin, Ripple is a private company that is creating a payment and exchange network (RippleNet) on a distributed database ledger (XRP Ledger). Ripple's core purpose is to connect banks, payment service providers and digital asset exchanges, making global payments faster and more cost-effective.

The history of Ripple

Ripple was created in 2004 by Ryan Fugger, who developed the first prototype of Ripple as a decentralized digital money system (RipplePay). The system was inaugurated in 2005 and aimed to provide secure payment solutions within a global network.

In 2012, Fugger sold the project to Jed McCaleb and Chris Larsen, who founded the American technology company OpenCoin. Since then, Ripple has started to be developed as a protocol focused on payment solutions for banks and other financial institutions. In 2013, OpenCoin was renamed with the Ripple Labs brand, turning into Ripple in 2015.

The XRP Ledger

Building on Fugger's work and inspired by the creation of Bitcoin, in 2012 Ripple introduced the Ripple Consensus Ledger (RCL), along with its native cryptocurrency XRP. The RCL was later renamed XRP Ledger (XRPL).

XRPL acts as a distributed economic system that not only keeps all the accounting information of the network participants but also offers exchange services between different currency pairs. Ripple presents XRPL as an open source distributed ledger that allows for real-time financial transactions. These transactions are protected and verified by the network participants through a consensus mechanism.

However, unlike Bitcoin, XRP Ledger does not rely on a Proof of Work consensus algorithm and, as a result, does not use a mining process to verify transactions. The network achieves consensus through the use of a custom consensus algorithm. This algorithm is formerly known as the Ripple Protocol Consensus Algorithm (RPCA).

XRPL is managed by a network of independent validation nodes that constantly compare their operation logs. Anyone can start and manage a Ripple validation node and choose which nodes to trust as validators. However, Ripple recommends its customers to use a list of identified and trusted participants to validate their transactions. This list is known as the Unique Node List (UNL).

The nodes of the UNL transfer transaction data between them until everyone agrees on the current state of the register. In other words, transactions that are accepted by a large majority of UNL nodes are considered valid and consensus is reached when all of these nodes add the same set of transactions to the ledger.

According to the official website, Ripple is a private company that funded the development of XRPL as an open source distributed ledger. This means that anyone can contribute to the code and that XRPL would be able to continue even if the company ceases to exist.

RippleNet

Unlike XRPL, RippleNet is exclusive to the Ripple company and was developed on top of XRPL as a payment and exchange network.

RippleNet currently offers a 3-product suite designed as a payment system for banks and other financial institutions. These products are xRapid, xCurrent, and xVia.

xRapid

In short, xRapid is an on-demand liquidity solution that uses XRP as an intermediate currency between different fiat currencies. Both XRP and xRapid are based on the XRP Ledger, which offers faster confirmation times and much lower rates than conventional methods.

Let's make a simple example. Bob is in Australia and wants to send $100 to Alice in India. Bob transfers the money through a financial institution called FIN. To carry out the transaction, FIN uses the xRapid solution to create a connection with exchanges in the countries of origin and destination. By doing so, the company is able to convert Bob's $100 into XRP, providing the necessary liquidity for the final payment. Within seconds, XRPs are converted to Indian Rupees and Alice can withdraw the money from an exchange in India. As you can imagine, if Bob and Alice followed the standard path of wire transfers, the transaction would have been much slower and more expensive.

xCurrent

xCurrent is a solution developed to provide instant transaction settlement and international payment tracking between RippleNet members. Unlike xRapid, the xCurrent solution is not based on the XRP Ledger and does not use the XRP cryptocurrency by default.

xCurrent is built on the Interledger Protocol (ILP), designed by Ripple to connect different registers or payment networks.

The four basic components of xCurrent are the following.

- **Messenger**. xCurrent messenger provides peer-to-peer communication between financial institutions connected through RippleNet. It is used to exchange information relating to risk and compliance, rates, exchange rates, payment details and expected times for the disbursement of funds.

- **Validator**. Validator is used to cryptographically confirm the success or failure of a transaction, as well as to coordinate the movement of funds in the Interledger. Financial institutions can run their own validator or rely on a third party.

- **ILP Ledger**. The Interledger Protocol is implemented within existing bank registers, creating the ILP Ledger. The ILP Ledger acts as a sub-ledger and is used to track credits, debts and liquidity through the parties carrying out transactions. Funds are settled automatically.

- **FX Ticker**. The FX ticker is used to define the exchange rates between the parties to the transactions. It monitors the current status of each configured Ledger ILP.

Even though xCurrent was designed primarily for fiat currencies, it also supports cryptocurrency transactions.

xVia

xVia is a standardized API-based interface that allows banks and other financial service providers to interact within a single facility, without having to rely on various payment network integrations. xVia allows banks to create payments through other credit partners connected to RippleNet, and also allows them to attach invoices or other information to transactions.

While Bitcoin is known as the open cryptocurrency and Ethereum is famous for creating a global smart contract platform, we can consider the Ripple network as a monetary exchange system that focuses on global payment solutions for banks and other financial institutions.

RippleNet can be implemented on top of the existing banking infrastructure as a means to complement and improve the traditional payment system. xCurrent allows for cost-effective and real-time payments through financial institutions, xRapid uses XRP as an intermediate currency to provide on-demand liquidity funds, and xVia facilitates the integration and communication of all RippleNet participants.

Chapter 4

Flare and Spark (FLR)

Flare is a distributed network with some unique properties. It can be used to build two-way bridges between networks, such as Ethereum and XRP Ledger. This means that it allows you to use the XRP token within smart contracts.

Spark Token is Flare's native token. A portion of the offering will be distributed to XRP holders through an airdrop.

As you should know by now, Ripple's XRP Ledger (XRPL) is a global payment and exchange network. Being optimized for this use case, it offers limited utility with regards to other kinds of functionality.

This is what the Flare Network aims to solve by introducing smart contract support for the XRP token.

Spark is the native token of this network, and a portion of its offering will be distributed to eligible XRP holders. Let's find out how it works.

What Flare Network is

The Flare Network is a distributed network that integrates the Ethereum Virtual Machine (EVM). Essentially, the EVM converts smart contracts into instructions that computers can read. This allows the network to execute complete Turing smart contracts. This attribute means that it can perform virtually any computational task, as long as there is enough memory to do so.

As a result, it can combine important properties to create an ecosystem of decentralized applications. In short, Flare aims to offer scalability for smart contract networks.

Flare uses a consensus protocol called Avalanche, which has been adapted to work with the Federated Byzantine Agreement (FBA). FBA is a consensus mechanism used by networks like XRPL and Stellar.

We won't go into detail in this chapter, the point is that Flare's consensus algorithm doesn't rely on economic mechanisms like Proof of Stake to maintain network security.

You may be wondering, what are these economic mechanisms? Let's take for example a token like ether (ETH) for the Ethereum network. When Ethereum completes its Proof of Stake (PoS) transition with Ethereum 2.0, network security will completely depend on validators staking their tokens. This means that, by extension, security will depend on the token. The consensus protocol implemented by Flare does not provide for this measure.

Why should this be emphasized? Because it allows the network token to be used for other kinds of applications. Even some that would be dangerous for networks that rely on the token for security. In practice, according to the creators of Flare, this design choice adds greater versatility to the token without compromising its security.

What is FLR?

Spark is the native token of the Flare Network. Its basic use case is similar to that of other native tokens, preventing spam attacks. If the transactions were free, even spamming and congesting the network with useless transactions would cost nothing.

Additionally, Spark Token can be used for the following features:
- As a collateral in decentralized applications (dApps)
- To provide data to an on-chain oracle
- To participate in the governance of the protocol

These three components aim to enable an ecosystem of Spark-based applications called Spark Dependent Application (SDA). Additionally, SDAs allow trustless representations of tokens on other networks, even those that do not natively support smart contracts. Are you starting to guess where we are getting? Yes, this is where XRP comes in.

What is the FXRP token?

FXRP is a trustless representation of the XRP token on the Flare Network. It can be created and redeemed by XRP owners through smart contracts.

The system relies on participants pledging Spark Token as collateral and earning commissions for creating and redeeming FXRP. This, combined with potential arbitrage opportunities, should ensure that the 1: 1 ratio between XRP and FXRP is maintained.
We mentioned that Flare allows you to use smart contracts on networks that don't support them. This is exactly the goal of FXRP. It allows XRP to be used in smart contracts without the need for a central authority to issue wrapped tokens. In other words, in a trustless way.

The Flare Network is a new scaling solution for networks that don't support smart contracts. Flare allows you to use XRP in smart contracts in a trustless way.

Chapter 5

Monero (XMR)

Public blockchains are inherently transparent. For blockchains to work in a decentralized environment, each participant must be able to independently verify all of their transactions. A quick glance at Bitcoin or Ethereum is enough to see how public their databases are.

Such an infrastructure offers several benefits, but it often does so at the expense of privacy and anonymity. Observers can link transactions and addresses in the blockchain to potentially deanonymize address owners.

These so-called pseudonymous cryptocurrencies are useful for a myriad of applications. However, privacy coins may be more desirable for those seeking true financial privacy. And when it comes to private cryptocurrencies, few have the same reputation as Monero.

What is Monero?

Monero is a cryptocurrency created according to the principles of non-associability and non-traceability. In simpler terms, this means that it shouldn't be possible to link two Monero transactions, nor to determine the source or destination of the funds.
This is what sets Monero apart from the rest of cryptocurrencies. It always uses a blockchain to track the movements of funds, but applies an interesting cryptographic scheme to obscure the sources, amounts and destinations of transactions.

A brief history of Monero

Monero is a fork of Bytecoin, a privacy-oriented cryptocurrency released in 2012. Bytecoin was the first protocol based on CryptoNote, an open source technology with the aim of solving some of the flaws of

Bitcoin. We are referring to ASIC mining and the lack of privacy in transactions. CryptoNote now forms the basis of many cryptocurrencies that want to value confidentiality.

In 2014, developers dissatisfied with Bytecoin's initial distribution forked the coin into a new project known as Bitmonero. Later, the name was changed in Monero.

How does Monero work?

While researching Monero, it is easy to come across the terms "ring signature" and "stealth addresses". These are two of the main innovations behind the anonymity of Monero's transactions. In this chapter, we will provide an overview of both concepts.

Ring signatures and confidential transactions

A ring signature is a type of digital signature created by someone in a specified group. With the signature and public keys of the group members available, anyone can verify that one of the participants provided the signature. However, it is not possible to understand which of these provided it.

In 2001, the "How to Leak a Secret" document illustrated this concept using the example of a government cabinet. Suppose a member of this cabinet - Bob - has incriminating evidence on the Prime Minister. Bob wants to prove to a reporter that he really is a cabinet member, but he wants to remain anonymous.

Bob would not be able to do this with a normal digital signature. Comparing it to his public key, anyone could confidently claim that only Bob's private key could have produced the signature. He could suffer serious consequences for spying on the Prime Minister's activities. However, by using the keys of the other cabinet members in a ring signature scheme, it will not be possible to determine which of them sent the message. However, it will be possible to say with certainty that the information comes from a cabinet member, thus proving its authenticity.

This technique is used every time you create a transaction, giving you anonymity. During the construction of the transaction, your Monero wallet takes other users' keys from the blockchain to form a ring. These keys actually act as diversions. To an observer, it will appear that anyone in the ring may have signed your transaction. Consequently, a stranger will never be able to determine whether an output has been spent or not. At best, they may know that one of the eight outputs shown in the image below may have been spent. We call the number of diversion outputs mixin.

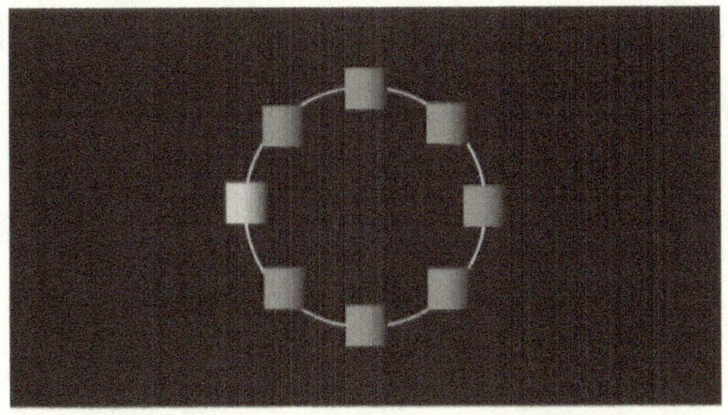

In the image above, the green output is what you are really spending, and the red ones are the diversions you have collected from the blockchain.

In the past, the outputs included in the ring had to be the same size. Otherwise, it would have been easy to understand what was going on, as the transaction amounts were visible. For example, you might have seen a ring that included only 2 XMR outputs or one where only 0.5 XMR outputs were included.

The update to RingCT (Ring Confidential Transactions) changed that. It has integrated confidential transactions, a technique in which transaction amounts are not visible. This integration into the Monero protocol has been a big boost in terms of privacy. You can now build a ring with outputs of various sizes without revealing information that could be used to de-anonymize you.

Stealth addresses

Ring signatures hide where the funds are coming from, but with regular public addresses you would still be able to see where they are going. This could be problematic if your identity is linked to one of your blockchain addresses.

Let's say we use the same address in our e-commerce store for every order. Anyone who buys on our site can see the balance we have and tell others that this is our business address. This could make us a target.

Stealth addresses hide the destination of funds. Essentially, the sender generates a one-time address based on a public address used only for that transaction. The public address might look like this:

41mT1gUnYHK6mDAxVsKeB7SP9hVesbESbWcupd7mMYC73GL4nSgsEwTGKHGT7GKoSEdMKvs8Fdu1ufPJbo5BV4d1PfYiEew

If you search for the address in a Monero block explorer, you will see that you cannot link any transactions to it. When a sender wants to send you funds, they create a stealth address by passing the above address through some math function. When they send XMR, they send it to a new address on the blockchain. Each address created will be different from the previous one, and cannot be connected to it.

However, there are two pieces of information you can use: the "view private key" and the spend private key. As the name indicates, the "view key" allows you to see all transactions associated with your address. You can give it to others to check the funds you have received. The spend key is what we usually think of as our private key. You use it to spend your coins.

Monero has a default privacy policy, meaning you can't decide not to use a stealth address. Therefore, while the public ledger is automatically blacked out, you can still make your transactions transparent to participants of your choice.

Monero vs. Bitcoin

Monero and Bitcoin have some similarities, but in reality they both have many unique aspects. Let's take a look at them.

Fungibility

Fungibility is a source of controversial discussions in the field of Bitcoin. It refers to the interchangeability of an asset with another asset of a similar type. Gold, for example, is considered fungible because you can trade one ounce of your own for someone else's, and this will be functionally identical. The same goes for coins and banknotes. You can exchange one ten-dollar bill for another. On the contrary, a unique masterpiece like the Mona Lisa is not fungible as there is no other similar unit.

In many digital currencies, determining fungibility appears to be more complicated. Bitcoin units are fungible at the protocol level, as the software makes no distinction between units of BTC. The situation becomes more ambiguous on a social and political level. Some argue that Bitcoin is not fungible because each output is unique, while others argue that this doesn't matter.

Since the Bitcoin blockchain is transparent, transaction details, such as amounts and recipients, can be tracked. Suppose you receive a five-dollar bill as change in a grocery store. Ten transactions prior to this, the note may have been used in a criminal transaction, which would have no effect on its current usability. With Bitcoin, we have seen occasions where some coins have been rejected or confiscated based on their "dirty" history. Even if users are unaware of previous transactions, surveillance services that analyze the blockchain can blacklist certain coins and affect their usability as a currency. And this is why some consider Bitcoin a non-fungible asset.

The "clean" coins, i.e. those that have just been mined, could be seen as more valuable than the old and "dirtier" ones.

Opponents of coin profiling believe that this practice uses unreliable and subjective techniques for analysis. In fact, several tools for mixing and CoinJoining are increasingly accessible to average users, and allow you to obfuscate the source of your funds.

Monero eliminates these problems right from the start. Since observers cannot know where the funds are coming from or where they are going, it is perhaps more like cash than non-privacy coins can be. Even in businesses with strict analytics policies, XMRs from suspicious transactions can be traded without any problems.

Monero's added privacy comes at a price though. Transactions are much larger. Therefore, there are major hurdles to overcome before the system can expand and scale to accommodate the masses.

Curiously, its strong fungibility has given the cryptocurrency a certain degree of notoriety, surpassing Bitcoin as the currency of choice for cybercriminals involved in cryptojacking, ransomware and dark web transactions.

Blocks and mining

Like Bitcoin, Monero uses Proof-of-Work to add transaction blocks to the blockchain. However, like all CryptoNote-based protocols, it is designed to be ASIC-resistant. The goal of this property is to prevent domain mining pools that use specialized high-performance hardware mining.

Monero's Proof-of-Work algorithm aims to make the system fairer by favoring CPU mining and weakening the effectiveness of GPUs. The rationale behind this measure is that mining will be better distributed as common PCs continue to be competitive. Despite this, hashing power remains relatively concentrated in a handful of mining pools.

As for the block size, Monero does not have a fixed limit, unlike the 4 million units by weight of the Bitcoin block. Instead, it has a dynamic block size. This means blocks can expand to accommodate greater demand. Likewise, if demand falls, the permitted size will decrease. The dimensions are calculated considering the average size of the previous hundred blocks. Miners can produce blocks that exceed the limit, but will be penalized with a reduced reward.

Importantly, the supply is not limited, as is the case with Bitcoin. Monero also has a decreasing block reward program, but it doesn't tend towards zero. Instead, the subsidy will remain indefinitely at a fixed amount to incentivize participants in block mining.

Hard fork

We find another interesting difference between Bitcoin and Monero at the governance level. Bitcoin is quite averse to forks, to the point that even simple updates remain under discussion for a long time before being implemented. But there is a reason for this. In fact, Bitcoin developers have to be cautious to ensure the system remains stable, secure, and decentralized.

Of course, forks are just protocol update mechanisms. They are often needed to fix critical bugs or to add new features. However, in Bitcoin users prefer to avoid them as they can cause divisions, and could pose a threat to decentralization. Typically, Bitcoin hard forks emerge when a group wants to create a new cryptocurrency from the existing network. Outside of this, they are usually reserved for emergency cases where urgent vulnerabilities need to be addressed.

In the case of Monero the roadmap has frequent hard forks. This ensures that the software can quickly adapt to changes and integrate security updates. Some see "mandatory" protocol updates as a weakness, even though Monero's hard forks don't carry negative connotations like other cryptocurrencies. This does not mean that they are foolproof. In fact, frequent hard forks increase the risk of undetected vulnerabilities, and can push out-of-date users off the network.

Monero development

Monero development is open to everyone. Anyone can contribute to the source code and documentation. The community decides which features to add, remove or modify. At the time of writing, the project has more than 500 collaborators. The Core development team is made up of developers such as Riccardo Spagni (aka FluffyPony), Francisco Cabañas (ArticMine) and the pseudonymous devs NoodleDoodle, Othe and binaryFate.

In addition to sponsorships, the development is funded by the Community Crowdfunding System. Users can propose ideas which, if selected by the community, follow a crowdfunding period. When certain milestones are reached the funds are distributed to the managers.

For years, Monero has been the go-to cryptocurrency for those looking for strong privacy guarantees. It has a dedicated community of developers who work to increase the confidentiality of user transactions. The new updates aim to further the mission of providing non-associable and non-traceability in cryptocurrencies.

We have invested in XRM in 2017 and we are holding it for the long term. We encourage you to look into it, as it is a pretty interesting project.

Chapter 6

Binance Smart Chain (BSC)

Binance Chain was launched by Binance in April 2019. Its primary goal is to facilitate fast and decentralized trading. Perhaps un-surprisingly, the largest decentralized application built on top of it is Binance DEX, one of the most accessible decentralized exchanges on the market. You can use it through a web interface at binance.org or through its native integration with Trust Wallet.

However, due to the inherent limitations of blockchain-based systems, Binance Chain does not have much flexibility to introduce smart contracts into a system optimized for real-time trading that could significantly congest the network. Have you heard of CryptoKitties? At the peak of its popularity, it brought the Ethereum blockchain to complete paralysis.

Scalability remains one of the most important challenges for blockchain development. And this is where Binance Smart Chain comes into play.

What is Binance Smart Chain?

Binance Smart Chain (BSC) can be described as a blockchain operating in parallel with Binance Chain. Unlike the latter, BSC offers smart contract functionality and compatibility with the Ethereum Virtual Machine. The design goal was to leave Binance Chain's high capabilities intact while introducing smart contracts into its ecosystem.

In essence, both blockchains operate side by side. BSC is not a layer two or off-chain scaling solution, but an independent blockchain that can work even if the Binance Chain goes offline. That said, both systems bear a strong design similarity.

Since BSC is compatible with EVM, it was launched with support from the rich universe of Ethereum tools and dApps. In theory, this makes it easier for developers to transfer their projects from Ethereum. For users, it means that applications like MetaMask can be easily configured to work with BSC. Seriously, it's just a matter of changing a couple of settings.

How Binance Smart Chain works

Binance Smart Chain achieves 3 second block times with a Proof-of-Stake consensus algorithm. Specifically, it uses a model called Proof of Staked Authority (or PoSA), where participants staking BNB to become validators. If they propose a valid block, they receive the transaction fees included in it.

Unlike many protocols, rewards are not distributed in newly issued BNB, as BNB is not inflationary. Conversely, the supply of BNB decreases over time as the Binance team carries out coin burns periodically.

Cross-chain compatibility

Binance Smart Chain was conceived as an independent system but complementary to the existing Binance Chain. Dual-chain architecture is used, to allow users to easily transfer assets from one blockchain to another. In this way, Binance Chain can offer fast trading, while powerful decentralized apps can be built on BSC. With this interoperability, users have a vast ecosystem at their disposal that can accommodate a number of use cases.

Binance Chain's BEP-2 and BEP-8 tokens can be exchanged for BEP-20 tokens, the new standard introduced for Binance Smart Chain.
To move tokens from one chain to another (from BEP-2 to BEP-20 or vice versa), the easiest method is to use the Binance Chain Wallet, available on Chrome and Firefox.

Decentralized Finance on Binance Smart Chain

You may already know that several digital assets - such as BTC, LTC, ETH, EOS and XRP - already exist on Binance Chain as "Peggy coins." These are tokens anchored to assets on their respective native chains. For example, you might decide to block 10 BTC in order to receive 10 BTCB on the Binance Chain. At any time, you can trade your 10 BTCB for 10 BTC, so the BTCB price should closely follow that of the native BTC.

By doing so, you are effectively transferring these assets to the Binance Chain. This is a type of tokenization and you should be familiar with this concept if you have read the dedicated chapter.

Thanks to the flexibility offered by the Binance Smart Chain, assets from a number of different chains can be used in the emerging DeFi industry. For example, applications like PancakeSwap allow users to trade assets trustlessly, participate in yield farming, and vote on proposals. Similar projects include BurgerSwap and BakerySwap.

Binance Smart Chain vastly expands the functionality of the original Binance Chain and joins a number of cutting-edge protocols designed to bridge the gap between different blockchains. While still in its early stages, the platform is an ideal engine for developers who want to build useful decentralized applications.

Chapter 7

Staking BNB on the Binance Smart Chain

Binance Smart Chain allows you to use the unlimited DeFi infrastructure at low cost. It is managed by a set of 21 community validator nodes that process transactions, provide processing power and hardware, ensuring network security. In return, they receive rewards from BNB's transaction fees and staking.

The purpose of the validators is to make BSC a bigger and more accessible ecosystem.

Validators

Binance Smart Chain uses a consensus model called Proof of Staked Authority (PoSA). It is a hybrid between the Proof of Authority (PoA) and the Delegated Proof of Stake (DPoS). This consensus model supports faster block times, lower fees, and ultimately requires only 21 validators to run.

Validators take turns producing the new blocks, feeding the BSC network through transaction processing and signing the blocks. In exchange for their service, they earn a reward in BNB tokens. In the meantime, they need daily re-election in order to continue being part of the set of validators; this is based on the amount of BNB they hold in stake.

What are the requirements to become a validator? A validator must maintain a node with the required specifications, manage a full BSC node and stake at least 10,000 BNBs. But that is not all. These requirements are only sufficient to become an elected candidate.

To actually start producing new blocks, a validator candidate must become a selected validator. The selected validators are the first 21 candidate validators with the most voting power. They change every 24 hours through a continuous election process and you can check them on the list of top validators on Binance.org.

What is a delegate on Binance Smart Chain (BSC)?

Becoming a validator isn't for everyone, so how can you participate as an ordinary user? Well, you can become a delegate and stake your BNBs to candidate validators using one of the supported wallets. Through staking, you can choose your favorite validators and help them achieve the minimum stake requirements required by the protocol.

In short, you are pooling your BNBs with your favorite validator. As we know, validators receive a reward in BNB. In exchange for the staking vote, the validator shares a portion of their earnings with their delegates. Therefore, we have a win-win situation for both parts.

Furthermore, delegates can transfer part of their staked BNB to another validator. This process is called redelegation. Redelegation is a great way to support multiple validators at the same time.

Delegates can also de-stake their BNBs. This function is called undelegate. As you guessed, this eliminates the delegation towards the selected validators. Note that the un-delegation requires an unbonding period of 7 days, at the end of which the delegate receives the BNBs that they had staked. During this phase the delegate does not receive any reward in BNB.

Should you become a delegate on Binance Smart Chain (BSC)?

The choice is yours. By becoming a delegate, you are delegating your staked BNBs to your favorite validator. Additionally, you are entrusting them with your voting power to approve or disapprove governance decisions. Furthermore, validators can control certain functionalities on BSC, such as adjusting gas prices, changing system parameters or even updating the blockchain.

By delegating your BNB to a validator, you will also increase its stake in relation to the total reward pool. Both of you, by joining forces, earn advantages and a reward. As of February 2021, the average daily reward for a validator on BSC was 134 BNB. Meanwhile, the average APR for delegates on BSC was 60%.

While the economic incentives are great and make everything work smoothly, being a delegate isn't all about returns. By becoming a delegate, you are directly supporting BSC's operations and security.

How to become a validator on Binance Smart Chain (BSC)

To become a BSC validator, you must meet these requirements:

- have powerful hardware;
- run a full node BSC;
- stake at least 10,000 BNB.

This will allow you to enter the list of candidate validators and potentially attract more delegates to stake their BNBs to your validator node.

As of April 2021, the top 21 elected validators all have more than 150,000 BNB staked. Therefore, there will be a lot of competition in the coming months, as the price of the BNB token increases.

How to become a delegate on Binance Smart Chain (BSC)

Becoming a delegate is probably the best choice if you want to avoid all the technical aspects of the validator. If you are a BNB owner, delegating your stake can be a simple solution to supporting BSC and earning a profit.

You can check out these guides on how to stake your BNBs using the most popular wallets:

- Binance Chain Wallet
- Trust Wallet
- MathWallet

Stake interest is distributed to the delegate every day after 00:00 UTC. When you delegate your stake to a validator, you will start receiving rewards the second day after delegating.

As of April 2021 the best validator has an APR of 27%. Not bad, but remember that rewards can fluctuate over time.

Whether you are a developer, a user or just a DeFi enthusiast, there are many ways to participate in the development of the BSC ecosystem. BNB staking is a great way to participate in BSC as a direct advocate of network health and safety.

We stake our BNB tokens with different validators and they have proved to be a nice source of income. We definitely recommend this practice.

Chapter 8

BakerySwap

BakerySwap is a DeFi protocol developed on Binance Smart Chain that offers interesting rewards. It works as a decentralized exchange by adopting the automated market maker model.

You've probably seen a ton of food-themed projects in the DeFi industry before. All of these protocols share one feature: users provide liquidity and earn tokens as a reward.

While many may associate DeFi with the Ethereum blockchain, more and more projects are being launched on Binance Smart Chain due to its minimal fees and faster confirmation times.

In this chapter, we will take a look at BakerySwap. It is a decentralized exchange built on the Binance Smart Chain.

What BakerySwap is

BakerySwap is a decentralized exchange that adopts the automated market maker model popularized by Uniswap.

BakerySwap is one of the first projects to leverage BSC to develop a DEX AMM. Furthermore, it is one of the few DeFi projects on Binance Smart Chain to offer liquidity pools for altcoins.

As with other platforms that use the AMM model, there is no order book to match buyers and sellers. Instead, users trade against a liquidity pool. The assets in each pool are provided by BakerySwap supporters and users.

Users who add liquidity to these pools receive liquidity provider tokens in exchange, based on their share of the pool. Later, they can convert these LP tokens to the original tokens they provided. The amount received also depends on the respective share of the pool. As a reward for the liquidity provided, they earn trading fees.

The BAKE farming process

As you'd expect from a platform called BakerySwap, the native token is called BAKE. You can earn it by staking BAKE, or by providing liquidity to one of the pools and staking your liquidity pool tokens.

For example, if you provide liquidity to the DOT-BNB pool, you will receive DOT-BNB BLP tokens. After that, you can stake these BLP tokens to receive BAKE. If you want to simply buy BAKE on the market instead of farming it, you can do it as well. Let's take a deeper look at the platform.

BakerySwap's liquidity pools

On BakerySwap, BAKE token stakers can explore pastry-themed menus. If you select Bread, you can stake BAKE to earn more BAKE. Alternatively, you can stake matching BLP tokens in pools, such as Donuts, Waffles, Rolls, Croissants, and so on. Remember that the potential ROI is different for each option.

As of April 2021, supported BEP-20 liquidity pools are the following.

- Bread: Staking by BAKE to earn BAKE
- Donut: Staking of BAKE-BNB BLP to earn BAKE
- Waffle: Staking by BAKE-BUSD BLP to earn BAKE
- Rolls: BUSD-BNB BLP staking to earn BAKE
- Croissant: Staking of BAKE-DOT BLP to earn BAKE
- Milk: USDT-BUSD BLP staking to earn BAKE
- Toast: Staking ETH-BNB BLP to earn BAKE
- Cake: Staking BTC-BNB BLP to earn BAKE

How to use BakerySwap

When you visit the BakerySwap website, you need to connect an eligible wallet to unlock all features. We recommend using MetaMask. MetaMask is an Ethereum wallet, but it can support Binance Smart Chain and its dApps with ease.

Once everything is set up, you can unlock the wallet to reveal additional information on the website.

Adding liquidity

The process of adding liquidity to BakerySwap is not very different from that of Uniswap or similar platforms. First of all you need to add liquidity to the DEX and provide both tokens to participate in that specific liquidity pool. Once liquidity is provided, you can start farming with BAKE.

To add liquidity, click on Exchange in the top menu and select the Pool tab. Then, click the "Add Liquidity" button.

Now, select the token pair you want to provide liquidity to. For example, you can select BNB and BAKE, so you will receive BAKE-BNB BLP tokens in return.

Once you have received your BLP tokens, you should navigate to "Earning" and select the option that corresponds to your BLP tokens. In this example, you will select Donut.

At this point, you should enter the amount of tokens you want to stake and confirm the transaction. Once completed, you can leave the page. You can come back at any time to see how many BAKEs you have earned. Received BAKEs are automatically collected when you withdraw the BLP token. Also, you can manually collect them by clicking on the Harvest button.

Other functions

We talked about the basic functionality offered by BakerySwap. But it doesn't stop there. There are other unique features to try.

One of these is the NFT marketplace, which allows you to buy non-fungible tokens.

Another unique feature is the BakerySwap Launchpad. It is a place where you can access newly launched projects on BSC. However, unlike Binance Launchpad, these are not "normal" tokens, they are NFTs.

The first Initial Dex Offering (IDO) was Battle Pets, a blockchain-based fighting game where players can breed, trade, and compete with NFT animals on the Binance Smart Chain.

The BakerySwap NFT Combo pool

In addition to this, BakerySwap allows you to create special menus called NFT Combo. These tools require you to lock BAKE and involve a bit of randomness. The more BAKE you block, the higher the class of NFT Combo you can create. These combos give you more and more Staking Power to earn more BAKE by farming your BLP tokens.

You can break them down at any time and take back 90% of the blocked BAKEs to create them. However, at the time of writing, all NFT Combo have been sold.

There are four classes of NFT Combo, and each requires a different amount of BAKE.

- Basic: 10,000–20,000 BAKE
- Regular: 20,000–50,000 BAKE
- Luxury: 50,000–100,000 BAKE
- Supreme: Over 100,000 BAKE

Remember, the Staking Power you receive for each combo is unique. It is based on the amount of BAKE you have blocked and a random multiplier. Therefore, the more BAKE you block, the higher your Staking Power potential will be.

Is BakerySwap Safe?

So far, there have been no reported problems with BakerySwap. An audit of the BakerySwap smart contract has been carried out and no issues were found.

However, depositing funds into a smart contract is always risky, as there may be bugs that went unnoticed during the audit. Never deposit money that you cannot afford to lose.

Whether you want to trade BEP-20 tokens, earn passive income with BAKE staking, or create special NFT Combo, BakerySwap offers you a ton of options.

Chapter 9

5 BSC Parameters to Keep an Eye On

We have talked about how public block-chains are permissionless, meaning that anyone with an address can interact with it. A less discussed feature is the fact that blockchain development is also permissionless. Anyone with the relevant skills can launch their dApp on a blockchain, and no one can stop it.

This leads to rapid development in the field of decentralized finance. Binance Smart Chain is only a few months old, but it is already seeing significant growth. There is a large amount of on-chain data available to the public, so it's easy for traders and investors to scrutinize the network's activity.

BscScan was developed by the same team that created EtherScan. It is a blockchain explorer and analytics platform for Binance Smart Chain, but it also has many other useful features. These can be great sources of information if you want to keep an eye on the DeFi on BSC.

In this chapter we take a look at five interesting parameter you should keep an eye on.

Yield farms on Binance Smart Chain

Yield farming is a way to generate crypto with your existing funds. Using platforms like PancakeSwap, you can generate returns on the Binance Smart Chain. As we will see with the next parameter, the commissions on BSC are extremely low. This makes the network ideal for smaller participants who want to enter the yield farming scene and reap some of the gains offered by the tools available.

The BscScan yield farming dashboard shows you all the current opportunities in this area. You can quickly access the latest farms and see information on what they do and how they work on dedicated websites. This should be the easiest bookmark ever if you are one of BSC's hard working farmers.

Another great resource for monitoring all the various dApps in the BSC ecosystem is https://mathdapp.store/. Just select Binance Smart Chain from the left menu and you will get a list of trusted dApps on BSC.

The average price of gas on the Binance Smart Chain

As we have mentioned in previous chapters, BSC has extremely low fees. On BSC, 1 gwei corresponds to 0.000000001 BNB.

With an average gas price of 20 gwei, sending 10 BNB equivalent to about $300 should cost around $0.01. Sending ten or even times that much shouldn't cost you more than a few cents. From the transaction history, we can see that some trades have paid higher fees. Some users may have reverted to their old habits on Ethereum or other compatible tools. It is not necessary. Binance Smart Chain is a long way from congestion, so 20 gwei should be enough.

The number of unique addresses on the Binance Smart Chain

BSC is cheap, but how can we roughly estimate how many users are on the blockchain? The number of unique addresses is a great way to start.

Does this mean that if a 100 unique address blockchain must have 100 unique users? Absolutely not. Anyone can create multiple addresses. And in any case, it would be rather difficult to find out if these addresses belong to the same entity.

So, we know that anyone can create multiple addresses, and this parameter is an overestimate. However, the number of unique addresses can give us a rough idea of the growth of the network.

Best BEP-20 Tokens

The Token Tracker page allows you to track the best BEP-20 tokens in terms of market capitalization or daily trading volume. This gives an idea of which tokens have the highest overall value on BSC, and which ones are experiencing the highest trading volumes.

One thing to keep in mind in this case is the token information. Those who manage tokens / smart contracts can update the information available on BscScan to provide more details regarding the token. If the token is not verified by the BscScan team, it may not be trusted.

You will see a lot of wrapped tokens on this page. For example, Binance-Peg ChainLink (LINK), i.e. LINK ERC-20 tokenized as BEP-20 token on BSC. What does wrapped mean? These assets are tokenized versions of a coin or token that belongs to another blockchain. This system allows you to use coins and tokens that are not present on BSC in Binance's DeFi ecosystem. For example, if you own LINK and want to use your tokens in yield farming on BSC, you can do so without selling them.

If you want to experiment with wrapped tokens, we encourage you to check out the Binance Bridge Project. Remember that while tokenizing a coin is a relatively easy process, it's not always necessary. You can simply exchange wrapped tokens that have already been tokenized by other people without worrying about the wrapping process.

Binance Smart Chain validators

To put it simply, validators are the participants who guarantee the BSC operation. Through BNB staking, they process transactions and confirm new blocks. In exchange for their services, they earn transaction fees from their network activity.

Binance Smart Chain is based on a consensus mechanism called Proof of Staked Authority. This consensus model can support minimal block time and low fees. You can see the main Binance Smart Chain validators by visiting the Validators Leaderboard.

Virtually anyone can become a validator, but the requirements are relatively high. After all, network security is at stake.

Whether you are a DeFi veteran or a complete beginner to yield farming on BSC, these metrics can help you improve your strategy for monitoring activity on Binance Smart Chain.

However, remember that markets are irrational, unpredictable and prone to periods of extreme volatility. Conducting your own research is critical to success in trading or yield farming. Among other steps to take, you can check if a token is verified by the BscScan team. If the smart contract is open source and has been checked, then you can visit the project's blog or social media accounts to learn more about it. Make sure you understand the risks associated with participating in DeFi before you risk your capital.

Chapter 10

Facebook Libra (DIEM)

Libra (renamed Diem) is a payment system proposed by Facebook. It is based on a permissioned blockchain intended to support an ecosystem for digital payments and other financial services.

Its currency, called Diem (originally known as Libra), will be backed by a basket of stablecoins and is scheduled to launch in 2021. But what else do you need to know about Facebook's cryptocurrency? Let's find out together in this chapter.

Digital payments are an industry with many opportunities. More and more people have access to the internet via smartphones, and much of the economic activity takes place online. Companies like

PayPal, Visa and MasterCard already handle a lot of this business. Furthermore, many projects in the crypto sector are trying to build products for this sector.

However, unlike other projects, Facebook already has a large user base. Well, big might be an understatement. In the third quarter of 2020, Facebook had approximately 2.7 billion monthly active users. This could potentially make their payment system an instant hit.

What is Facebook Libra (Diem)?

Libra (renamed Diem) is a blockchain-based payment system proposed by Facebook in 2019. Its goal is to provide access to financial services for people without a bank account. Founding members include Morgan Beller, David Marcus and Kevin Weil.

The launch was originally scheduled for 2020, but has been postponed for various reasons and will likely take place in 2021.

Libra will be governed by the Libra Association (renamed the Diem Association), an independent association based in Geneva, Switzerland. The members of the association are various companies from the blockchain, tech, payments, telecommunications, venture capital and non-profit sectors.

Libra Association members are responsible for governance decisions, overseeing the operations of the Libra payment system and the projects developed on the Libra blockchain. Facebook aims to have 100 members in this association before the launch of Libra.

Is Libra a cryptocurrency?

Well, Libra is based on a blockchain, and it uses cryptographic technology. However, the term cryptocurrency usually implies specific properties that Libra does not possess. In short, it would be more correct to call Libra a digital currency.

How will Facebook Libra work?

The Libra Blockchain (renamed Diem Blockchain) is a permissioned blockchain that forms the backbone of this payment system. But what distinguishes it from other blockchains?

We have talked about permissionless blockchains such as those of Bitcoin or Ethereum. This means that anyone with an internet connection can freely access them, transact or develop on them. There is nothing and no one controlling access.
However, in the case of a permissioned blockchain the situation is quite different. To use it, you need permission from whoever is controlling the network. More precisely, the applications you use will need to have special access.

The fact that Libra is a permissioned blockchain also means that it doesn't use mining or staking to validate transactions like many other blockchains. Instead, it will rely on a group of authorized validators to validate transactions. These validators are the members of the Libra Association.

According to its creators, after the first five years Libra could turn into a Proof of Stake system. However, this is a very long time in such a nascent industry. So why not use PoS right from the start? Libra's white paper explains the reasons behind this decision. In their view, there is currently no permissionless system that can support the business of billions of people.

Is Facebook Libra decentralized or centralized?

According to many in the blockchain industry, permissioned blockchains cannot have the same degree of decentralization as their permissionless counterparts, as they are more like a traditional corporate database.

In this sense, Libra is not as resistant to censorship as Bitcoin and other cryptocurrencies. Since these validators must be members of the Libra Association, the network could end up being relatively centralized. On the other hand, controlling and verifying which applications can interact with the distributed ledger can have its advantages. For example, it may be easier to rule out malicious applications and scams.

The Libra payment system

Libra payment system supports several single currency stablecoins pegged to fiat currencies, such as USD, EUR, GBP. These work in a similar way to the stablecoins you may already know, in that their value is derived from a reserve called the Libra Reserve. This reserve consists of cash, cash equivalents and short-term government bonds.

Additionally, the Libra payment system will also support a multi-currency coin called Diem Dollar (ticker symbol LBR). It is a sort of a combination of all the other stablecoins in the system, and is backed by a basket of assets that ensures its value. You can think of it as a stablecoin of stablecoins. The idea is that these various forms of collateral can protect users from volatility. This is an important aspect for something that aims to act as a form of payment.

The Libra cryptocurrency can be stored in an incoming wallet called Novi (formerly Calibra Wallet). As expected, this digital wallet could be integrated into other social media products, such as Facebook Messenger and WhatsApp. According to the plans, users should be able to easily convert between US dollars (or other fiat currencies) and Facebook's currency.

Libra's source code, called Diem Core, is open source and written in Rust. Everyone can see the code directly on Diem's GitHub page. According to plans, Libra will also support smart contract functionality through a programming language called Move.

Facebook Libra and Bitcoin

At this point, it is evident that Libra and Bitcoin are fundamentally different and may very well coexist in the future. While both can be considered digital payment systems, they aim to serve different use cases.

Bitcoin is a decentralized and censorship-resistant cryptocurrency that often serves as a reserve asset or store of value. Libra, on the other hand, is a proposal based on a permissioned network that suggests a more centralized model.

The future of Libra

Facebook has received several criticisms following the original Libra announcement, mostly from central banks, lawmakers and regulators. It remains to be seen whether they will manage to combine all the elements necessary to make Libra a successful project.

We are excited about Libra and we look forward to using it. Of course, since its price is going to be stable, you cannot consider it an investment.

Chapter 11

Bitcoin ETF

Bitcoin and the cryptocurrency market have come a long way. A decade ago, this technology was only used by a small community of enthusiasts. In this period the price was around 10,000 BTC for two pizzas.

In just a few years we have seen several successful companies make their way in this sector, we have seen the development of many new cryptocurrencies, the birth of DeFi and much more. On top of all this, institutional adoption is also growing. MicroStrategy has converted more than $2 billion of its balance sheet into Bitcoin and you may soon be able to buy the latest Tesla model with your BTC.

What key steps are missing before Bitcoin can become an important asset in the global macroeconomic environment? One of these could be a regulated instrument that allows traditional institutions and traders to gain exposure to BTC. According to some, the best way would be via an ETF.

What is a Bitcoin ETF?

Let's start from the definition. An ETF is an exchange traded fund, which is an investment fund that tracks the price of an underlying asset. ETFs are used in various sectors and for different types of assets. For example, gold ETFs have been around for decades and track its price.

A Bitcoin ETF would work the same way. The ETF's price would follow Bitcoin's.

ETFs are regulated financial products, which are traded on traditional markets such as the NASDAQ or NYSE and not on a cryptocurrency exchange. This situation could change in the future, as the boundaries between traditional finance and the cryptocurrency industry are getting closer and closer.

The importance of a Bitcoin ETF

Bitcoin is not the easiest asset to manage. For example, custody can cause major headaches for a large institution. After all, Goldman Sachs won't just link a hardware wallet to a PC and "YOLO" $ 2billion in Bitcoin. Large financial institutions do not operate in the same way as individual investors; they need a complex regulatory framework flanked by a financial system to be able to move in this sector.

This is why an ETF can make a difference in broadening adoption and potential investor base. It could offer exposure to traders in traditional markets, without the latter having to worry about everything needed to physically own the coins.

A Bitcoin ETF could also contain other assets besides BTC. For example, a Bitcoin ETF could contain a basket of other assets such as Bitcoin, Ethereum, Tesla shares, gold, and so on. This would lead to diversification useful for investors.

A brief overview of Bitcoin ETFs

Generally, when we talk about Bitcoin ETFs, we usually talk about ETFs on US markets. However, ETFs exist in many other markets. For example, the first Bitcoin ETF was launched on the Canadian stock market. It is called the Purpose Bitcoin ETF and is traded on the Toronto Stock Exchange under the BTCC ticker.

The focus is currently on US regulators, as the US financial market is the largest in the world. A US Bitcoin ETF could consolidate Bitcoin as an investment asset.

There have been several attempts to launch a Bitcoin ETF in the United States. As of March 2021, they have all been rejected by the US Securities and Exchange Commission (SEC).

Why does the SEC keep rejecting such regulatory requests? These are the arguments for denying the claims of a Bitcoin ETF: the volatility, the unregulated nature of the Bitcoin markets and the apparent vulnerability of the latter to market manipulation. While these arguments may be plausible to some extent, the fact remains that the same could be true for many other financial markets that already have an ETF.

Furthermore, much of the financial structure required to legitimize Bitcoin as a macro asset class was built during the last bear market. If MicroStrategy, just a few years ago, had wanted to buy billions of dollars in Bitcoin, it probably would have been very difficult. Now, both the infrastructure and the liquidity are mature enough to be able to manage even such substantial investments.

Probably, the continuous evolution of the Bitcoin market will change the cards on the table for the regulatory bodies, so as to lead to the possible birth of a US Bitcoin ETF. It's hard to say when it will happen but it may be sooner than we think.

Should you invest in a Bitcoin ETF?

Is a Bitcoin ETF the right financial tool to invest in Bitcoin? Well, if your intention is to protect your savings from devaluing fiat currencies, it might be best to buy Bitcoin directly.

After all, Bitcoin is democratized finance. Having direct custody of your savings can be very useful. Not to mention the countless ways you can earn an annuity or borrow, using your Bitcoins as collateral.
That said, there are also advantages to a Bitcoin ETF, if you find them interesting, in this case an ETF can also be a good choice.

A Bitcoin ETF allows traditional market investors to gain exposure to Bitcoin in a regulated manner. It can be a good way to achieve more institutional adoption of the crypto world as an asset class. When will US regulators agree to issue a Bitcoin ETF in the US? It is difficult to say, but it seems that all the pieces are falling into place.
We will not invest in a Bitcoin ETF, because we believe that it is much better to own your BTC directly.

Chapter 12

Earning with Crypto: Staking

In the next few chapters we are going to talk about some of the methods cryptocurrency offer to earn passive income on your investments. We strongly believe that a good crypto portfolio has a part dedicated to dividend yielding, especially now that standard interest rates are near 0.

You can think of staking as an alternative to mining that requires the use of fewer resources. It involves holding funds in a cryptocurrency wallet to support the security and operations of a blockchain network.

Simply put, staking is the act of blocking cryptocurrencies to receive rewards.

In most cases, you will be able to stake your coins directly from your crypto wallet, such as Trust Wallet or MetaMask. Additionally, many exchanges offer staking services to their users. Binance Staking, for instance, allows you to earn rewards in an extremely simple way. In fact, all you have to do is keep your coins on the exchange. This is another reason why we love Binance so much.

To better understand staking, you will first need to understand how Proof of Stake works. PoS is a consensus mechanism that allows blockchains to operate with greater energy efficiency while maintaining a decent degree of decentralization

A look at PoS

Proof of Work has proven to be a very robust mechanism for facilitating consensus in a decentralized context. However, the problem is that it involves a great deal of arbitrary computation. The puzzle that miners compete to solve has no other purpose than to keep the network secure. It could be argued that this in itself makes over-computation justifiable. At this point, you may be wondering: are there no other ways to maintain decentralized consensus without the high computational cost?

Proof of Stake is the answer to this question. The central idea is that participants can block coins, and at particular intervals, the protocol will randomly assign one of them the right to validate the next block. Typically, the likelihood of being chosen is proportional to the amount of coins. This means that the more coins you block, the higher your odds.

In this way, what determines which participants create a block is not based on their ability to solve hash problems like in Proof of Work. Instead, it is determined by how many coins they hold in staking.

Some might argue that block production through staking allows for a greater degree of scalability for blockchains. This is one of the reasons why the Ethereum network has planned a migration from PoW to PoS in a set of technical updates collectively known as ETH 2.0.

The inventor of Proof of Stake

One of the first Proof of Stake appearances can be attributed to Sunny King and Scott Nadal in their 2012 paper for Peercoin. They describe it as a "peer-to-peer cryptocurrency design derived from Satoshi Nakamoto's Bitcoin."

The Peercoin network was launched with a hybrid PoW / PoS mechanism, where the PoW was mainly used to issue the initial supply. However, it was not necessary for the long-term sustainability of the network, and its importance was gradually reduced. In fact, much of the network's security was based on PoS.

Delegated Proof of Stake

An alternative version of this mechanism was developed in 2014 by Daniel Larimer called Delegated Proof of Stake or DPoS. It was first used as part of the BitShares blockchain, but shortly after other networks adopted the model. These include Steem and EOS, also created by Larimer.

DPoS allows users to commit their balances as votes, where the voting power is proportional to the number of coins in their possession. These votes are then used to elect a number of delegates who run the blockchain on behalf of their constituents, ensuring security and consensus. Typically, staking rewards are distributed to these elected delegates, who distribute part of the rewards to their constituents in proportion to their individual contributions.

The DPoS model allows consensus to be achieved with fewer validation nodes. Because of this, it tends to improve network performance. On the other hand, it can also result in a lesser degree of decentralization as the network relies on a small select group of validation nodes. These nodes manage the operations and the governance of the blockchain. They participate in the processes to reach consensus and define fundamental governance parameters.
In other words, DPoS allows users to report their influence through other network participants.

How staking works

As we have already discussed before, Proof of Work systems rely on mining to add new blocks to the blockchain. On the contrary, Proof of Stake networks produce and validate new blocks through the staking process. Staking consists in the freezing of coins by validators in order to be randomly selected by the protocol at specific intervals to create a block. Usually, participants who stake a larger stake have a higher chance of being chosen as the next block validator.

This allows you to produce blocks without relying on specialized mining hardware, such as ASICs. While ASIC mining requires a significant investment in hardware, staking requires a direct investment in the cryptocurrency itself. Therefore, instead of competing for the next block with computational work, PoS validators are selected based on the number of coins they are staking with. The "stake" is what motivates validators to maintain network security. If they don't, their entire stakes could be at risk.

While each Proof of Stake blockchain has its own particular staking currency, some networks adopt a two-token system where rewards are distributed using the second token.

On a very practical level, staking simply means holding funds in a suitable wallet. This allows anyone to perform various functions for the network in exchange for staking rewards.

Calculating staking rewards

Each blockchain network can use a different way to calculate staking rewards.

Some methods are regulated on a block-by-block basis, taking several factors into consideration. These can include:

- how many coins the validator has in staking
- how long the validator has been actively staking
- how many coins are staking on the network in total
- the rate of inflation

However, for some networks staking rewards are determined as a fixed percentage. These rewards are distributed to validators as a kind of inflation compensation, which encourages users to spend their coins instead of keeping them, potentially increasing their use as cryptocurrencies.

A predictable rewards program can be beneficial for someone. Furthermore, considering that the reward percentage is made public, it could incentivize more participants to take part in the staking process.

Staking pools

A staking pool is a group of coin holders who pool their resources to increase the odds of validating blocks and receiving rewards. They combine their staking power and share rewards proportionally to individual contributions to the pool.

Creating and maintaining a staking pool often takes a lot of time and expertise. Staking pools tend to be most effective on networks where the barriers to entry are relatively high. For this reason, many pool providers charge a commission on the staking rewards distributed to participants.

Additionally, pools can provide greater flexibility to individual stakers. Typically, the stake must be locked for a fixed period and usually has a withdrawal or dissolution period set by the protocol. Furthermore, a substantial minimum balance is almost always required for staking, with the aim of discouraging malicious behavior.

Most staking pools require a low minimum balance and do not impose additional withdrawal times. Therefore, joining a staking pool instead of staking alone might be ideal for new users.

Cold staking

Cold staking refers to the staking process on a wallet that is not connected to the internet. This can be done using a hardware wallet, but it is also possible with an air-gapped software wallet.

Networks that support cold staking allow users to stake while securely storing their funds offline. It is important to note that if the owner moves their coins out of cold storage, they will no longer receive the rewards.

Cold staking is particularly useful for large holders who want to ensure maximum protection of their funds and support the network at the same time.

Our favorite coins to stake are KAVA, ADA and BNB. Once ETH 2.0 will be released, we will stake our ETH as well.

Chapter 13

Yield Farming

The second method you can use to earn passive income on your cryptocurrency is called Yield Farming and in this chapter we are going to tell you everything you need to know about it.

The decentralized finance movement has been at the forefront of innovation in the blockchain industry. DeFi applications are permissionless, so anyone with an internet connection and a supported wallet can interact with them. Furthermore, they usually do not require trust in any third party. In other words, they are trustless.

One of the new concepts that emerged from this area is yield farming. This is a new way to earn rewards using cryptocurrency funds through permissionless liquidity protocols. It allows anyone to generate passive income using the decentralized ecosystem built on Ethereum. For this reason, yield farming may change the way investors hold their coins in the future.

What yield farming is

Yield farming, also known as liquidity mining, is a way to make money using cryptocurrency funds. Simply put, it means blocking cryptocurrencies to receive rewards.

From a certain point of view, yield farming can be compared to staking. However, there is much more complexity in the background. In many cases, it involves users called liquidity providers (LPs) who add funds to liquidity pools.

A liquidity pool is a smart contract that contains funds. In exchange for the liquidity provided to the pool, liquidity providers receive a reward, which can be composed of commissions generated by the underlying DeFi platform or from other sources.

Some liquidity pools distribute the rewards in different tokens, which can be deposited into other liquidity pools to earn from there as well, and so on. You can already imagine how incredibly complex strategies can emerge. However, the basic idea is that a liquidity provider deposits funds into a liquidity pool and receives rewards in return.

Yield farming usually takes place on Ethereum with ERC-20 tokens, and rewards are paid in an ERC-20 token. However, this may change in the future. Why? Because in the future cross-chain bridges and other similar advances could allow DeFi applications to become independent of a particular blockchain. This means they could run on other blockchains that support smart contract functionality.

Typically, yield farmers often shift their funds from one protocol to another in search of high yields. As a result, DeFi platforms could provide other economic incentives to attract more capital as well. As with centralized exchanges, liquidity tends to attract more liquidity.

What triggered the yield farming boom?

The sudden and strong interest in yield farming can be attributed to the launch of COMP, the governance token of the Compound Finance ecosystem. Tokens of this type confer governance rights to the holders. But how to distribute these tokens to make the network as decentralized as possible? Well, a common way to start a decentralized blockchain is to distribute these governance tokens algorithmically, with liquidity incentives. This represents an incentive for liquidity providers to "farm" the new token by providing liquidity to the protocol.

While it didn't invent yield farming, the launch of COMP gave a big boost to this token distribution model. Since then, other DeFi projects have come up with innovative schemes to attract liquidity to their ecosystems.

The Total Blocked Value (TVL)

The Total Blocked Value (TVL) is a metric that measures how many cryptocurrencies are stuck in loans and other types of DeFi money markets.

In a sense, TVL represents aggregate liquidity in liquidity pools. It is a useful index for measuring the health of DeFi and the yield farming market as a whole. Furthermore, it is an effective benchmark for comparing the "market share" of the different DeFi protocols.

To monitor the TVL we can use Defi Pulse. On Defi Pulse you can see which platforms have the most ETH or other crypto assets locked in DeFi. This should give you a general idea of the current state of yield farming. Of course, the greater the locked-in value, the greater the ongoing yield farming activity. It is worth noting that it is possible to measure TVL in ETH, USD or even BTC. Each will offer a different perspective on DeFi's money market conditions.

How yield farming works

Yield farming is closely tied to a model called the automated market maker or AMM.

Liquidity providers deposit funds into a liquidity pool. This pool is used by a marketplace where users can lend, borrow, or trade tokens. Using these platforms incurs fees, which are then distributed to liquidity providers based on their share of the liquidity pool. This is the basic structure of how an automated market maker works.
However, the implementations can be very different. We should never forget that it is a new technology. We will certainly see the launch of new approaches that bring improvements to current implementations.

In addition to fees, another incentive to add funds to a liquidity pool could be the distribution of a new token. For example, a project could create a system where the only way to receive its token is by providing liquidity to a specific pool, as this is not available in the open market.

The rules of distribution depend entirely on the implementation of the protocol. The key point is that liquidity providers receive a reward based on the amount of liquidity they provide to the pool.

Deposited funds are usually USD-pegged stablecoins. However, this is not a strict requirement. Among the most popular stablecoins in DeFi we find DAI, USDT, USDC, and BUSD. Some protocols issue tokens that represent the coins deposited in the system. For example, if you deposit DAI in Compound, you will receive cDAI, or Compound DAI. If you deposit ETH in Compound, you will receive cETH.

As you can imagine, there can be different levels of complexity in this context. You could deposit your cDAIs in another protocol that issues a third token to represent your cDAIs, which in turn represent your DAIs and so on. These chains can become very complex and difficult to follow. We will not get into the more complex yield farming strategies, as we do not use them.

Calculating yield farming yields

Typically, yields from yield farming are calculated on an annual basis. The estimates thus obtained represent profits generated over a year.

Some commonly used parameters are the annual percentage rate (APR) and the annual percentage yield (APY). The difference between the two is that the APR does not consider the effects of compounding, while the APY does. Compounding, in this case, indicates the process of directly reinvesting profits to generate more returns. However, be aware that in some cases APR and APY may be used interchangeably.

It should also be remembered that we are only talking about estimates and projections. The actual rewards are quite difficult to accurately estimate. In fact, yield farming is a highly competitive and fast-paced market, and the rewards can fluctuate quickly. If a yield farming strategy works for a while, several farmers will take advantage of the opportunity, and the returns obtained from it will be lower.

Since APR and APY derive from traditional markets, DeFi may have to find its own parameters to calculate returns. Due to the fast pace of the industry, it may be more useful to estimate weekly or even daily returns.

DeFi and collateralization

Typically, you need to provide collateral to borrow assets. Basically it acts as insurance for your loan. Depending on which protocol you decide to provide funds to, you may need to keep an eye on collateralization.

If the value of your collateral falls below the limit required by the protocol, it could be liquidated on the open market. To avoid this scenario, you can add more collateral.

Each platform has a particular set of rules for this process and a different collateralization ratio required. Furthermore, on most of these platforms we find a concept called "overcollateralization". This means that borrowers have to deposit more value than they want to borrow, to reduce the liquidation risk following violent market crashes.

For instance, suppose the loan protocol you want to use requires a collateralization ratio of 200%. This means that for every $100 of value you provide, you can borrow $50. However, it is usually safer to add more collateral than required to further reduce the liquidation risk. That said, several systems use high collateralisation ratios to keep the entire platform relatively safe from liquidation risk. The collateral can even reach 750% of the borrowed amount.

Risks of yield farming

As you can imagine, yield farming isn't easy. The most profitable strategies are extremely complex and indicated only for expert users. Additionally, yield farming is generally more suitable for those with a lot of capital to invest.

This practice is not as simple as it sounds, and if you don't understand what you are doing you will probably end up losing money. We talked about the liquidation danger on your collateral, but there are risks you need to know before getting started with yield farming.

An obvious risk of yield farming involves smart contracts. Given the nature of DeFi, many protocols are created and developed by small teams with limited budgets. This can increase the risk of bugs in smart contracts.

Even in the case of larger protocols verified by reputable auditors, new bugs and vulnerabilities are often found. Due to the immutable nature of the blockchain, this can lead to a loss of user funds. Take this into account when blocking your funds in a smart contract.

Furthermore, one of the main advantages of DeFi is also one of its greatest risks: the concept of composability. Let's examine its impact on yield farming.

As already mentioned, DeFi protocols are permissionless and can be easily integrated with each other, so the entire DeFi ecosystem is heavily dependent on each of its building blocks. This is what we mean when we say such applications are composable. They can work together easily.

The problem arises when one of the elements doesn't work as expected, and the entire ecosystem suffers. This is one of the biggest risks for yield farmers and liquidity pools. Not only do you have to trust the protocol you deposit your funds into, but also all the others that that protocol depends on.

Yield farming platforms and protocols

What is the best way to make money with yield farming? This question has no definitive answer. Yield farming strategies can change in a matter of hours. Each platform and strategy has its own set of rules and risks. If you want to get started with yield farming, you first need to familiarize yourself with how decentralized liquidity protocols work.

You already know the basic idea. Deposit funds into a smart contract and receive rewards in return. However, implementations can vary widely, so it's generally not a good idea to blindly deposit your funds and hope for high returns. As a basic rule of risk management, you need to be able to stay in control of your investment.

That being said, let's take a look at some of the protocols that form the core of yield farming strategies.

Compound Finance

Compound is an algorithmic money market that allows users to lend and borrow assets. Anyone with an Ethereum wallet can provide assets to Compound's liquidity pool and earn rewards that immediately begin producing compound interest. Rates are adjusted algorithmically based on supply and demand. Compound is one of the central protocols in the yield farming ecosystem.

MakerDAO

Maker is a decentralized credit platform that supports the creation of DAI, an algorithmically anchored stablecoin to the value of the USD. Anyone can open a

Maker Vault to freeze collateral, such as ETH, BAT, USDC, or WBTC, generating DAI as debt against the blocked collateral. This debt accrues interest over time, called the stability fee. The rate of this fee is set by holders of MKR tokens.

Yield farmers can use Maker to issue DAI for use in yield farming strategies.

Synthetix

Synthetix is a protocol for synthetic assets. It allows the stake of Synthetix Network Token (SNX) or ETH as collateral against which to issue synthetic assets. Virtually anything that has a reliable price feed can be a synthetic asset. Therefore, any financial asset can be added to the Synthetix platform.
In the future, Synthetix could allow all sorts of assets to be used for yield farming. Do you want to use long-term gold investments in a yield farming strategy? Synthetic assets may be the solution.

Aave

Aave is a decentralized lending and borrowing protocol. Interest rates are adjusted algorithmically, based on market conditions. Creditors receive "aToken" in exchange for their funds. Upon deposit, these tokens immediately begin to accrue compound interest. Additionally, Aave offers other more advanced features, including flash loans.

As a decentralized lending protocol, Aave is widely used by yield farmers.

Uniswap

Uniswap is a decentralized exchange protocol that allows token exchanges in a trustless system. Liquidity providers deposit an equivalent value of two tokens to create a market. After that, traders can trade using this liquidity pool. As a reward for their service, liquidity providers earn commissions from the trades that take place in their pool.

Uniswap is one of the most popular platforms for trustless token swaps due to its user friendly nature. It can be a useful tool for yield farming strategies.

Curve Finance

Curve Finance is a decentralized exchange protocol designed specifically for efficient stablecoin swaps. Unlike other similar protocols like Uniswap, Curve allows users to swap large amounts of stablecoins with relatively low slippage.

As you can imagine, given the abundance of stablecoins in the yield farming landscape, Curve pools are a key part of the DeFi infrastructure.

Balancer

Balancer is a liquidity protocol similar to Uniswap and Curve. However, the key difference is that it offers custom token allocations in a liquidity pool. As a result, liquidity providers can create custom Balancer pools instead of following Uniswap's 50/50 allocation. Just like the latter, LPs earn commissions for transactions made in their liquidity pools.

Thanks to the flexibility it introduces in the creation of pools, Balancer is an important innovation for yield farming strategies.

Yearn.finance

Yearn.finance is a decentralized ecosystem of aggregators for loan services such as Aave, Compound and others. Its goal is to optimize token lending by algorithmically finding the most profitable services. After deposit, funds are converted into yTokens which rebalance periodically to maximize profits.

Yearn.finance is a useful tool for farmers looking for a protocol that automatically chooses the best strategies for them.
We absolutely love Yearn.finance and it is the main service we use to do yield farming.

Conclusion

ongratulations on making it to the end of this book, we hope you found some useful insights to take your cryptocurrency trading skills to the next level. As you should know by now, the world of cryptocurrency is extremely complicated and there is a new "opportunity" every way you look. However, our experience tells us that only by taking things seriously and having a proper plan you can develop your investing skills to the point that you can actually accumulate wealth.

Our final advice is to stay away from the shining objects that the world of cryptocurrencies offers you every day. Simply study the world of cryptocurrencies in depth and when you feel ready try to invest a little bit of money. Analyze your results, improve your money management skills and become the master of your emotions.

As you can see, there are no shortcuts you can take. Easy money does not exist. What exists is the possibility to start from zero and work your way up to become a professional cryptocurrency investor. The journey might be difficult, but it is certainly worth it.

To your success!